To
Dad
Christmas 2004

Lots of love from

Danny + Ann
xxxx

The Spitfire Story

Spitfire IX photographed during the filming of Piece of Cake at Charlton Park, Wiltshire, March 1988.

The Spitfire Story

Peter R. March

Sutton Publishing

Sutton Publishing Limited
Phoenix Mill, Thrupp, Stroud
Gloucestershire, GL5 2BU

First published 2006

Reprinted 2006, 2007

British Library Cataloguing in Publication Data
A catalogue for this book is available from the British Library.

ISBN 978-0-7509-4402-1

Typeset in 9.5/14.5pt Syntax.
Typesetting and origination by
Sutton Publishing Limited.
Printed and bound in England by
J.H. Haynes & Co. Ltd, Sparkford.

CONTENTS

ACKNOWLEDGEMENTS

It has been a difficult task to select photographs to illustrate *The Spitfire Story* from the huge number of excellent images that are available from a host of skilled photographers around the world. In the main I have chosen colour shots, often of contemporary aircraft, that show the outstanding features and grace of this beautiful warbird.

I am particularly grateful to Michael J.F. Bowyer, Peter Cooper/Falcon Aviation Photos, Dr Alfred Price, Brian Strickland and Richard L. Ward for making historic photographs available from their collections and to Derek Bower, Damien Burke, Ben Dunnell, Jeremy Flack/API, Darren Harbar, Paul Harrison, Jamie Hunter, Graham Kilsby, Andrew and Daniel March, Frank Mormillo, Richard Paver, Col Pope and Robby Robinson for the supply of more recent images.

Much has been written about the birth and development of the Spitfire. I gratefully acknowledge the assistance provided by Dr Alfred Price, the Spitfire Society, the Royal Aeronautical Society (Southampton Branch), Dr Gordon Mitchell and Michael J.F. Bowyer in the preparation of this book. I have also been ably assisted by Brian Strickland, Ben Dunnell and Howard Curtis in producing the narrative and appendices.

Photo Credits

Photographs Peter R. March/PRM Aviation Collection unless otherwise credited.

In the air the Spitfire was forgiving and without vice, and I never heard of anyone who did not enjoy flying it. It had a personality uniquely its own. The Hurricane was dogged, masculine and its undercarriage folded inwards in a tidy businesslike manner. The Spit, calling for more sensitive handling, was altogether more feminine, had more glamour and threw its wheels outward in an abandoned extrovert way. From the ground there was a special beauty about it. The cockpit of any single seater aircraft is a very snug private world, but to sit in the cockpit of a Spitfire, barely wider than one's shoulders, with the power of the Merlin at one's finger tips, was sheer poetry – something never to be forgotten by those who experienced it.

Lettice Curtis, Air Transport Auxiliary pilot.

Stephen Kettle's statue of R.J. Mitchell, with a model of the first Spitfire and a dismantled Mk 22 beyond, is on display at the Science Museum, South Kensington, London. (Science Museum)

If asked to name a British aircraft of the Second World War many people would pick the Spitfire. The subject of constant development, the Supermarine design was the RAF's most capable fighter of the period and was in front-line service throughout the war.

There can be no doubt that the basic concept and design of this beautiful fighter was pure genius. Reginald Mitchell and his colleagues such as Joseph Smith conceived an aircraft which was revolutionary in its time. Notwithstanding this achievement, the concurrent development of the Rolls-Royce Merlin and Griffon engines must equally be celebrated. The vision of the design team and the determination they showed in getting the aircraft off the drawing board and into the air can only be matched by Mitchell's bravery in the face of terminal cancer.

The Spitfire underwent continual development throughout the Second World War to maintain its place in the front ranks of the world's fighter aircraft. In six years of war the power of the Spitfire increased by 100 per cent, its weight by 40 per cent, its maximum speed by 35 per cent and its rate of climb by 80 per cent. Although the main line of development was as a fighter, the early introduction of photographic reconnaissance aircraft, and later the Seafire, gave rise to other separate types. The development of the Griffon engine as a replacement for the Merlin made a further main division, and finally there existed several interim types which bridged the gaps between one mark and the fully developed and strengthened mark that followed it. There were some combat aircraft which were faster power for power, or could carry a greater load, but none could

Did you know?
Although the final cost of the prototype Spitfire was £20,756, the Air Ministry paid £12,478 and Rolls-Royce £7,500, so in effect Supermarine built the aircraft at a cost to them of just over £700.

Did you know?

The average cost per aircraft of the first 310 Spitfires built was £6,033, reducing to £5,696 for the next 200. Today, if you wanted to buy an airworthy Spitfire you would have to find more than £1 million.

match the Spitfire in overall performance or ease of handling.

Forever remembered for its part in the Battle of Britain, the Spitfire took on the Luftwaffe's Messerschmitt Bf 109s in daily combat.

During the battle most of the fighter-versus-fighter combat took place between 13,000 and 20,000ft, because that was where German bombers normally flew. At that altitude the Mks I and II were about equal to the Bf 109E in capability. Over the next five years the Spitfire gained the equipment it needed for fighting a modern war – particularly armour plate and variable-pitch propellers that allowed maximum engine efficiency in all flight regimes, from the Merlins and Griffons. Spitfires flew on every operational front and took part in every major theatre of war, including Italy, Malta, the Middle East, India and Australia. As well as being a standard fighter in the RAF and Commonwealth air forces, it was also used by France, Poland,

◄
The classic shape of the Spitfire changed little through the Merlin-engined fighters like this Mk VIII, while the performance advanced significantly.
(Jamie Hunter)

Norway, the Netherlands, Yugoslavia, Belgium, Portugal and Russia. Over 700 were supplied to the US Army Air Force under the reverse of Lend/Lease.

Three or four new variants appeared in each year of production, and the final total built was 22,758 Spitfires and Seafires in 33 different marks. Few aircraft have rivalled its unique handling qualities, and it was unquestionably the finest fighter aircraft to come from the wartime British aircraft industry. It made the greatest single fighter contribution, alongside the Avro Lancaster bomber, to the outcome of the war in Europe.

After the war the Spitfire's front-line fighter role was fairly short-lived as the new generation of jet-powered Vampires and Meteors quickly took its place. But some aircrew brought up on Spitfires still hankered after its relative ease and simplicity.

Much of the enthusiasm for this classic fighter has been transmitted forward to the following generations. It remains, seventy years after its first flight, a truly great aircraft with a remarkable performance, an outstanding service record and a unique appeal to everyone who sees it in the air.

Peter R. March, January 2006

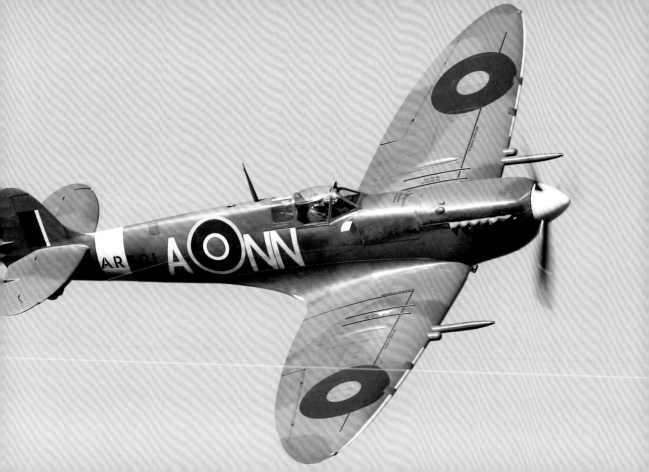

➤
The sleek racing lines of the Supermarine S6B, the forerunner of the Spitfire. It won the Schneider Trophy outright in 1931, setting the world air speed record in the process.

Did you know?

Spitfire designer R.J. Mitchell initially trained as an engineer with a locomotive firm in the Midlands before entering the aircraft industry. During his seventeen years with Supermarine he was responsible for the design of twenty-four different types of aircraft.

The Supermarine Spitfire was designed by R.J. Mitchell, a brilliant aircraft engineer who was born in Stoke-on-Trent in 1895. He incorporated into his new monoplane fighter the fruitful results of the experience gained in the design of a series of high-speed seaplanes from 1925. This culminated in the awesome Supermarine S6B racing seaplane which won the Schneider Trophy outright for Britain in 1931 and established three world air speed records. Mitchell's Supermarine Type 300 fighter showed the distinctive lines of the Schneider racers in its fuselage, but had a new elliptical-shaped wing. However, it was the emergence of the Rolls-Royce PV.12 engine – later named the Merlin – that was to be the most important catalyst in the new fighter's development. With the help of the Rolls-Royce team under E.W. (later Lord) Hives, the famous Merlin and Griffon engines were honed to perfection, together with propeller development, first by de Havilland and later by Rotol.

Built to a 1934 Air Ministry specification that called for an eight-gun fighter that could

The winning combination – Reginald J. Mitchell CBE and Sir Henry Royce at RAF Calshot in 1931.

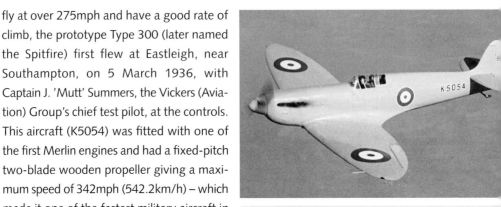

Captain 'Mutt' Summers
flying the prototype
K5054 on the day the
fighter was named
'Spitfire'. (via Dr Alfred Price)

The first Spitfire to arrive
on No 19 Squadron at
RAF Duxford in 1938,
being poked and prodded
by the ground crew
getting their first look at
the new fighter.
(via Dr Alfred Price)

fly at over 275mph and have a good rate of climb, the prototype Type 300 (later named the Spitfire) first flew at Eastleigh, near Southampton, on 5 March 1936, with Captain J. 'Mutt' Summers, the Vickers (Aviation) Group's chief test pilot, at the controls. This aircraft (K5054) was fitted with one of the first Merlin engines and had a fixed-pitch two-blade wooden propeller giving a maximum speed of 342mph (542.2km/h) – which made it one of the fastest military aircraft in the world at that time.

In a rare and inspired moment of foresight, the Air Ministry put its faith in this unproven design, an act which was to have great significance in the global conflict then brewing. The first order for 310 production Spitfire Is was placed on 3 June 1936 and exactly two years later the first deliveries were made to the RAF, entering service with 19 (F)

Line-up of No 19 Squadron's Spitfire Is during the press day at RAF Duxford on 4 May 1939.
(via Dr Alfred Price)

Did you know?

When the Air Ministry ordered 310 Spitfires from Supermarine in June 1936, it was the biggest single production order ever placed. By the end of production in 1948, 22,758 Spitfires and Seafires of 52 operational variants had been built.

Squadron at Duxford in July 1938. Sadly, Mitchell had died of cancer a year earlier aged just 42, never knowing how crucial his last aircraft would be to the defence of Britain over the next eight years.

At the outbreak of war ten RAF fighter squadrons (Nos 19, 41, 54, 65, 66, 72, 74, 602, 603 and 609) were equipped with Spitfire Is. On 16 October 1939 Spitfires of 602 and 603 Squadrons shot down a pair of Junkers Ju 88s off the coast of Scotland and on 28 October Flying Officer Archie McKellar of 602 Squadron shot down the first Luftwaffe aircraft to be downed on British soil, a Heinkel He 111. Production of Spitfires increased rapidly at a growing number of factories and by July 1940 there were nearly a thousand on the strength of nineteen RAF squadrons, at the start of the Battle of Britain.

Spitfire Is of 65 Squadron at RAF Hornchurch in 1939, with early refinements including three-blade propellers and modified cockpit canopies.
(via Brian Strickland)

'In the world of aircraft design the name of Mitchell is synonymous with that of the Spitfire, the outstanding fighter of [the Second World War]. In my written report on the combat I stated that in my opinion the Spitfire was superior overall to the Me 109, except in the initial climb and dive; however, this was an opinion contrary to the belief of the so-called experts. The Spitfire, with a better rate of turn than the 109, had the edge overall in combat. There may have been scepticism by some about my claim for the Spitfire, but I had no doubts on the score, nor did my fellow pilots on 54 Squadron. Later events, particularly in the Battle of Britain, were to prove me right.'

New Zealander Air Commodore Alan Deere, famous Battle of Britain pilot

Developments of the basic airframe and engine quickly followed, the team now led by Joseph Smith, who had succeeded Mitchell as chief designer. The Spitfire evolved to meet specific Fighter Command require-ments. Mks I and II were similar, the latter

This Spitfire IA with eight Browning machine-guns and a three-blade propeller was developed to meet specific Fighter Command requirements.

Did you know?

After the successes of the Schneider Trophy races Henry Royce received a knighthood – but Reginald Mitchell was only awarded a CBE. Unfortunately Mitchell had died by the time the Spitfire reached high acclaim and no retrospective award could be given.

to any combination of cannon/machine-guns. The subsequent 'E' wing fitted to the Mk IX in 1944 had the bigger 0.50in US Brownings. Other improvements included a larger rudder and for the Mk XVI a tear-drop canopy with a cut-down rear fuselage. When used for low-level (LF) fighter-bomber duties a clipped wing was standard. The

▲

Similar to the Mk I, the Spitfire IIA had a three-blade propeller and increased armour protection. Red tape across the gun ports on the leading edge shows the positions of the eight Browning machine-guns.

➤

The 'B' wing on this Spitfire VB incorporated 20mm cannon in place of the Browning machine-guns fitted to the VA.
(Daniel J. March)

having an improved Merlin engine, a three-blade propeller and increased armour protection; Mks V, VIII, IX and XVI were fighters or fighter-bombers powered by the Merlin 45 series (Mk V), the Merlin 60 series (Mks VIII and IX) or the Packard Motors-built Merlin 266 (Mk XVI) and fitted with redesigned wings to carry more fuel and 20mm cannon ('B' wing) in place of the Browning machine-guns ('A' wing) or the universal ('C' wing) which could be adapted

Mks VI and VII were high-altitude fighters powered by the Merlin 47 (Mk VI) and Merlin 60 series (Mk VII), both with a pressurised cockpit, retractable tailwheel and 'C' wing. The Mks IV, X and XI were unarmed photo-reconnaissance versions, with the Mk XIII being an armed variant. Over 18,300 Merlin-engined Spitfires were built.

◄
With a universal 'C' wing, this Spitfire VC could be adapted to accommodate any combination of cannon/machine-guns.

◄
A Spitfire LF.XVIE with its distinctive tear-drop canopy and cut-down rear fuselage leading an HF.VIIIC, which introduced a larger rudder. The Mk XVI had a Packard Motors-built Merlin and its 'E' wing had bigger 0.50in US Brownings.

A Spitfire LF.IXC with the six-gun 'C' wing carried over from the Mk V. When used as a low-level (LF) fighter-bomber, the Spitfire normally had clipped wings.
(Daniel J. March)

was basically a re-engined Mk VIII with a five-blade Rotol propeller and enlarged fin and rudder, 1,055 being built in 1943–4. Other Griffon-engined Spitfires were the Mks 21, 22 and 24 fighters/fighter-bombers and the Mk XIX unarmed photo-reconnaissance aircraft. The PR.XIX had a top speed of 460mph and a ceiling of 43,000ft.

Spitfires were also developed for the Fleet Air Arm, where they were known as Seafires. Initial versions were converted Spitfire VBs and VCs, the latter forming the basis for production Seafire IICs, of which 262 were built. The Seafire III was the first to feature folding wings. Development mirrored that of the Spitfire and Griffon-engined Seafires (Mks XV and XVII) were built by Westlands and Cunliffe-Owen during the war and the Mks 45–47 (RN equivalents of the Spitfire 21/22) followed after the war.

In 1943 the Rolls-Royce Griffon-engined Spitfire XII entered service with 41 and 91 Squadrons at RAF Hawkinge. The new power-plant increased the power, speed and rate of climb, particularly at low level. This was applied to good effect in the Mk XIV which

◄
Merlin-powered Spitfire PR.XI, an unarmed photo-reconnaissance version. It is painted in 'PR blue', the standard colour scheme for RAF high-altitude reconnaissance aircraft, and in this case over-painted with 'D-Day' invasion stripes.

➤

*To help avoid
interception from
German jet fighters,
Supermarine designed
this long-range unarmed
Spitfire PR.XIX
reconnaissance variant,
powered by a Rolls-
Royce Griffon engine. It
had a top speed of
460mph and a ceiling of
43,000ft.*
(Jamie Hunter)

➤➤

*The last piston-engined
fighter designed by
Supermarine; as the jet
age dawned, the Spitfire
F.24 brought the
development of the
land-based variants of
R.J. Mitchell's fighter
to a close.*

Through the war years the Spitfire was at the forefront of battle, but it was certainly not alone and, as the statistics show, it was not always an overwhelming success. During the Battle of Britain the early Spitfires could be outflown by the Luftwaffe's Messerschmitt Bf 109Es, particularly in a dive. The Spitfire scored on aesthetics, manoeuvrability and

'A common misunderstanding is to assume that the performances of the Hurricane and Spitfire were very similar. Test pilot Jeffrey Quill records that Dunkirk, as the first major test of the Spitfire in combat with fighters, was of the utmost importance. It showed the Spitfire's superiority in speed (Mk I Hurricane 311mph, Mk I Spitfire 355mph), rate of climb and turning circle. Mitchell's uncompromising search for performance in his design of the Spitfire was finally justified.'

Dr Gordon Mitchell, son of R.J. Mitchell

◄

Seafire IBs on the flight deck of a RN fleet carrier in 1943. Apart from the introduction of a retractable 'V' frame arrester hook, they were almost identical to the RAF's Spitfire VB counterpart.
(via Brian Strickland)

Did you know?

The Spitfire was the only Allied fighter to remain in full production from the first to the last days of the Second World War.

aerodynamic refinement and showed a greater potential for development than its opposite number. Unfortunately, the speed at which the enemy progressed its alternative fighter designs, such as the Focke Wulf Fw 190, could not be matched by the overstretched Supermarine team. Thus there was another period in 1941–2 when the enemy once again had the edge – at least until the Spitfire IXB entered service.

There can be little doubt that the Spitfire began to have much more of its own way from the latter half of 1943 onwards. Now it became a versatile, fast, well-armed fighter, demonstrating its flexibility in the low-level fighter, ground-attack and fighter-reconnaissance roles in particular. It is, quite naturally, from the last two years of the war that much of the folklore about the Spitfire is derived. Many more of the Spitfire pilots from this time were the 'survivors', who had memories of their successes against the Germans in Europe or the Japanese in the Far East. Not so the Seafire pilots, though. The Fleet Air Arm's adaptation of the Spitfire for carrier operations was never a great success. The Spitfire's relative weak, narrow-track undercarriage brought disaster to many an

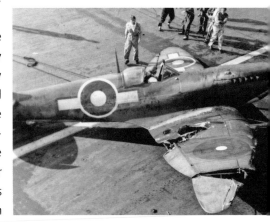

➤
Seafire III NN211 following a typical carrier landing accident.
(via Michael J.F. Bowyer)

unwary pilot as he bounced on to the heaving deck of a carrier. Until the arrival of the contra-rotating propellers of the Seafire 47, the torque swing from the powerful Griffon engine equally created problems on take-off or overshoot, causing some spectacular mishaps.

The last of 22,758 Spitfire variants was built in October 1947 and the famous fighter remained in RAF service until 1951, with a

> *'I think the simplest tribute I can pay this wonderful little aircraft is that from August 1940 until the end of war in Europe, except for six months' rest in 1943, I flew all types of Spitfires from Mk I to Mk XIV on well over 1,000 sorties against the Luftwaffe. Only on one occasion was I hit by enemy fire, and I never had to return to base through any mechanical trouble.'*
>
> Group Captain J.E. 'Johnnie' Johnson DSO and two bars, DFC and bar, DFC (USA).
>
> Johnson was the leading RAF ace with thirty-eight victories

final trio of PR.XIXs serving with the 'weather' flight at RAF Woodvale until 1957. In ten years of production and development, Mitchell's fighter progressed from the Spitfire I with a top speed of 355mph, maximum weight of 5,280lb and rate of climb of 2,500ft/min to the Seafire 47's 451mph, maximum weight of 12,500lb and climb of 4,800ft/min. The vision of that young designer and his team back in the 1920s in responding to the challenge of the Schneider Trophy enabled Britain to fight off (aided by the Hawker Hurricane) the apparently overwhelming Luftwaffe challenge in the dark days of 1940, and subsequently to match the best that Germany could produce in the shape of Messerschmitt Bf 109s and Focke Wulf Fw 190s in the following years.

ROLLS-ROYCE MERLIN

Originally known as the PV.12, the new Rolls-Royce engine that became the Merlin started as a private venture, since the Air Ministry had no funds available at the time. All Merlins were twelve-cylinder Vee-type engines with the two sets of cylinders arranged at an angle of 60 degrees. The cylinders were 'the right way up', being mounted above the crank, with a swept volume of 1,647 cu. cm (27 litres). The Merlin first appeared in 1933 and was basically a scaled-up Kestrel, but the cylinder block and cylinder head were integral as a one-piece casting. Instead of the water evaporative cooling system used on the earlier engines, the coolant was pure ethylene glycol and a conventional radiator was fitted.

An early modification was the fitting of a controllable-pitch propeller, while the

◄
A Rolls-Royce Merlin 45 removed from a Spitfire LF.VB, showing its two sets of six cylinders arranged in a Vee shape at an angle of 60 degrees. (Andrew P. March)

Did you know?

Only Rolls-Royce engines were fitted to the Spitfire – the Merlin and then the Griffon. Some Merlins were made under licence in the USA by the Packard automobile company and were fitted to some later marks of Spitfire.

21

Merlin II engine had a universal shaft capable of taking either the de Havilland or Rotol constant-speed propeller.

Increased power necessitated increased cooling, and progressive changes were made to the cooling arrangements in the wing culminating, at the introduction of the two-stage engine, in the use of duplex radiators, one side combining glycol and oil coolers and the other side glycol and intercoolers. As the power of the Merlin engine advanced, an increase in propeller 'solidity' also became necessary. With restrictions on the diameter due to ground clearance, four-blade propellers were required, followed by five blades for the more powerful Griffon engine. Eventually Supermarine adopted the idea of a contra-rotating propeller, which would, in theory, help to enhance performance.

Did you know?
It was the introduction of higher-grade octane petrol (100 against 87) in April 1940 that allowed the Spitfire's Rolls-Royce Merlin engines to run at a higher power, increasing the speed by 25–34mph.

ROLLS-ROYCE GRIFFON

On 8 November 1939, the Ministry of Aircraft Production expressed an interest in a Griffon II-powered version of the Spitfire. Rolls-Royce had developed an engine with the potential for even greater power.

The Griffon extended the performance of the Spitfire beyond that reached with the 60 series Merlin. This engine was 23 per cent bigger in capacity than the Merlin but broadly followed similar lines in terms of its mechanical features and superchargers. The Griffon had a lower thrust line than the Merlin, as well as being longer, resulting in a lengthier nose and projecting cylinder block. The Griffon's drive rotated in the opposite direction to that of the Merlin, but had a frontal area only 6 per cent larger. This necessitated a larger spinner, behind which a four or five-blade propeller was fitted. To accommodate this engine the front fuselage had to be redesigned and strengthened. The outcome was a cowling of better aerodynamic form than that on the Merlin version.

Rolls-Royce's ultimate Griffon 85 drove six-blade Rotol contraprops and was fitted to a few Spitfire F.21s and the Seafire F.47.

◄
The Rolls-Royce Griffon engine, as seen here in the open cowling of a PR.XIX, was 23 per cent bigger than the Merlin. Being longer, it resulted in a lengthier nose and projecting cylinder blocks.
(Robby Robinson)

The basis of the Spitfire's elliptical wing was an unusually robust torsion box leading edge, but it was rather expensive to manufacture.

The performance of the Spitfire came from the low drag of the thin elliptical wing, the slender form of its fuselage and the complete harmony of the parts that made the whole aircraft. Throughout its production life it was possible to step up the performance by adding more and more powerful engines, because the basic structural design was capable of ongoing development.

The basis of the wing was an unusually robust torsion box leading edge, which could be strengthened by increasing the thickness of the components. This torsion box took most of the wing loads and made it possible for the remainder of the structure to be light and, more significantly, allowed it to incorporate the armament, radiators and undercarriage.

The torsion box was bolted to the fuselage at the bottom of the fireproof bulkhead (firewall), on to which the engine mounting, with its heavy weight and power was hung. Two fuel tanks totalling 851 imperial gallons, with direct feed to engine pumps, were also situated close to the bulkhead. The small cockpit was set right back above the wing trailing edge. Thus the strength, weight and power were grouped together, so that increases in one or all of them had a localised effect. The narrow landing gear consisted of two Vickers cantilever oleo-pneumatic shock-absorber legs, which were raised outwardly into the underside of the wing. There was an emergency device for lowering the wheels in case of hydraulic system failure.

Standard Spitfire wings were elliptical on plan and tapered in thickness, and rather expensive to manufacture. Structure was chiefly of light alloy. The fuselage was of all-metal monocoque construction which

Did you know?

Of the Spitfires that were 'presented' during the war, just one, Mk IIB P8332 *Soebang*, donated by Queen Wilhelmina of the Netherlands, survives today at the Canadian War Museum in Ottawa.

consisted of channel section transverse frames and 'Z' section intercostals, four main longerons and a flush-riveted 'Alclad' skin. The after portion of the fuselage incorporating the tailfin and tailplane was detachable. The tail unit was of cantilever monoplane type with the fin integral to the rear portion of the fuselage. The elevator and mass-balanced rudder, both incorporating trimming tabs, had tubular ribs with (initially) fabric covering. This all resulted in a low structure weight of just 1,900lb at the prototype stage.

Apart from its lack of range, the least desirable feature of the Spitfire was its narrow track undercarriage. The closely spaced outward-retracting legs were very attractive from the designer's point of view (i.e. its cleanness when retracted, simplicity of the retracting mechanism and weight

Spitfire fuselages were of all-metal monocoque construction and featured transverse frames as clearly seen in this Mk IA under restoration.
(Graham Kilsby)

27

distribution) but it did not provide a very stable base. Thus the Spitfire was more prone to swing on take-off and to wallow when turned fast on the ground than an aircraft with a wider track. However, the Spitfire's generally excellent handling qualities compensated for this deficiency.

In early tests during high-speed dives it was discovered that pressure differentials made it impossible to slide the cockpit back in an emergency at over 250mph. Therefore a small knock-out panel was incorporated which, when pushed out, equalised the external and internal pressures. The cockpit was given a bulged hood providing more room and a better view for the pilot, and a thick slab of perspex was added at the front to make the windscreen bulletproof. The seat and bulkhead were given armour and the fuel tanks made self-sealing.

The government's initial order for Spitfires was increased to 510 in 1937, causing concern at Vickers-Supermarine's small factory on Southampton Water. Unlike the Hurricane, the Spitfire with its stressed skin

monocoque airframe, complex curvature and subtlety of line, was not well suited to mass production. Initially Supermarine built fuselages only, subcontracting out all other components (mainly in the Southampton, Salisbury, Reading and Trowbridge areas). In turn there was a large amount of detail work out-sourced to firms scattered around the country, who produced anything from wings to filler caps for fuel tanks. It quickly became apparent that a 'shadow' factory was essential and this was opened at Castle Bromwich, near Birmingham, where car manufacturers Nuffield handled the bulk of Spitfire production.

Did you know?

To escape the German bombers the manufacture of Spitfire components and sub-assemblies was moved to requisitioned premises in Southampton, Winchester, Reading and Trowbridge, including large garages, laundries, bus stations and steam-roller works.

The Spitfire factory at Itchen was destroyed by Luftwaffe bombers in September 1940.

Speed was the major consideration in fighter design, coupled with rate of climb, and there is little doubt that the main reason for the Spitfire's continued success was the progressive increase in speed, from the Mk I's 362mph to the Mk 24's 450mph, and its rate of climb from 2,500 to 4,800ft/min. So far as climb was concerned, efforts were mainly directed to reducing weight and choosing the right compromise in propeller design and gear ratio to suit the next stage of engine development. Extended wing tips were fitted in some cases and by this means the Spitfire's rate of climb was kept ahead of requirements.

It is also a fact that speed is a result of combining maximum power with minimum drag. So the policy adopted by the firm of making advance provision for engine development, and at the same time refining and reducing the drag of an already clean aerodynamic shape, paid a handsome dividend. Untiring efforts by Rolls-Royce resulted in the doubling of the Spitfire's engine power, from a maximum of 1,050hp on the Mk I to 2,350hp on the Seafire 47.

◄◄
The classic Spitfire's clean aerodynamic shape is illustrated by this Merlin-engined Mk IXB, which had a top speed of 408mph when it entered service in 1942.

COMPARATIVE PERFORMANCE

	SPITFIRE I	SPITFIRE IX	SPITFIRE XIV	SEAFIRE F.47
ENGINE	Merlin II/III	Merlin III	Griffon 65/67	Griffon 85/87
POWER	1,030hp	1,565hp	2,035hp	2,350hp
MAX. SPEED	362mph	408mph	439mph	452mph
	584km/h	657km/h	706.5km/h	727.5km/h

The first production
Spitfire I photographed in
May 1938, flown by test
pilot Jeffrey Quill. It had
a two-blade propeller
and a flat-topped cockpit
canopy.
(via Dr Alfred Price)

Although the range of Spitfire mark allocations runs from I to 24 it was by no means a straightforward matter of 24 marks. Two different types had the same mark number (III and PR.III and IV and PR.IV), one mark was renumbered (from IV to XX), two numbers (XV and XVII) were not used because they were reserved for Seafires, and another mark (F.23) was planned but not built. Complicating the family tree further were many variants and subvariants and different designations. Spitfires were also modified from one mark to another, for example the postwar conversion of two-seat Spitfire trainers from Mks VIII and IX to T.8 and T.9.

The Supermarine Type 300 **Spitfire i** had a 1,030hp Rolls-Royce Merlin II or III powerplant driving a fixed-pitch wooden propeller. Early improvements soon available included two-position controllable-pitch propellers and an engine-driven hydraulic pump. Production Spitfires had a more 'humpy' engine cowling than the prototype. New ejector exhausts were fitted, which provided some extra thrust to offset some of the humps. The first aircraft had a flush cockpit, but this was soon bulged on top as it restricted the height of the pilot and his view. The canopy slid to the rear and a hinged panel on the port side of the fuselage assisted entry and exit. The seat and rudder pedals were adjustable. When the Mk I entered service it weighed 5,280lb and had a maximum diving speed of 450mph.

Broadly similar, the **Spitfire II** was fitted with a 1,175hp Merlin XII engine driving a Rotol constant-speed three-blade propeller and had 73lb of armour plate. The Merlin XII differed in having a Coffman cartridge starter.

Did you know?
During the Second World War Supermarine produced both the fastest and the slowest operational aircraft for the Royal Air Force – the Spitfire and the Walrus amphibian.

'I would like an outfit of Spitfires in my group.'

So said Adolph 'Dolfo' Galland, noted Luftwaffe ace from JG.26, when asked by Reichsmarshall Herman Goering, who had underestimated Britain's air defences, what he needed to win the Battle of Britain in September 1940

➤

Mk IIAs retained the original eight machine-guns as early cannon armament had proved troublesome. (Derek Bower)

Did you know?

The first long-distance flight by a Spitfire was made on 29 October 1940 by a PR.ID photographing the Baltic port of Stettin, which required a flight of 5 hours 20 minutes.

In the Battle of Britain in 1940 it was soon realised that the two-position propellers fitted to the Spitfire were inadequate for climb and ceiling, although they fulfilled their original purpose of improving take-off performance. Subsequently either de Havilland or Rotol constant-speed variable-pitch propellers were fitted, improving the climb and ceiling. It was also realised that eight machine-guns alone were barely adequate, so a variant of the Mk II was produced with four improved Browning machine-guns, where the rate of fire was increased from 1,100 to 1,200 rounds per minute, and two 20mm cannon. The new type was known as the **Spitfire IIB**, while the original eight machine-gun version was retrospectively designated the **Spitfire iiA**. The cannon proved troublesome in early trials when the feed and ejector mechanisms jammed, and it was not until late 1940 that cannon-armed Spitfires performed satisfactorily in service.

Also in 1940 an attempt was made to improve the Spitfire's performance by 'clipping' the wing tips. At the same time a retractable (instead of a fixed) tailwheel was fitted. This **Spitfire III** was powered by a 1,260hp Merlin XX. It did not go into production.

'When I first flew the Spitfire I in action over Dunkirk in May 1940, and being very green in those days, I was enormously pleased with the speed at which it would dive in order to get a very frightened pilot out of trouble. The Spitfire has always looked good and handled beautifully after the introduction of metal ailerons. The cockpit and the sitting position have always been exactly right. It is a very satisfactory aeroplane to fly blind in cloud because of its inherent stability. Like most British fighters, it will stand a lot of punishment in the air.'

Group Captain Douglas Bader DSO and bar, DFC and bar, with twenty-two victories to his credit

The first photographic reconnaissance version, the **Spitfire PR.IV** was produced in 1941. A total of 229 of these fast, unarmed aircraft, powered by a 1,100hp Merlin 45 (and later 46, 50, 55A or 56) entered service. They were fitted with either one F52 vertical camera with a 36in lens, one F24 with a 14in lens or two 20in F8 cameras.

The **Spitfire V**, reputedly the best handling Spitfire of all, first went into service with 92 Squadron in the spring of 1941, and was the mainstay of Fighter Command during 1941 and 1942. It was fitted with a Merlin 45 rated at 1,440hp at 16,000ft, a Merlin 46 rated at 1,100hp at 19,000ft or a Merlin 50 or 50A. These engines featured

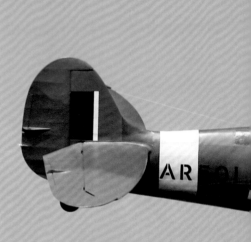

With its 'B' wing, the Spitfire VB was armed with two 20mm cannon and four machine-guns.

centrifugal superchargers developed by Stanley Hooker. With the Mk V the all-up weight increased to 6,417lb and the maximum level speed was now 369mph.

Originally there were three versions, differing only in armament: the **Mk VA** with eight 0.303in machine-guns; the **Mk VB** with four machine-guns and two 20mm cannon; and the **Mk VC** with 'universal' wings that could take either four cannon or two cannon

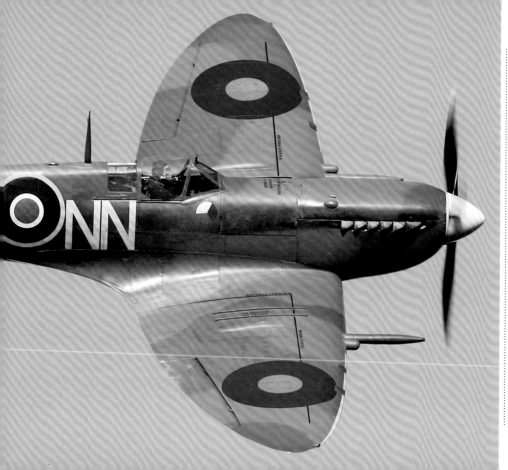

◄
Mk VCs featured the 'universal' wings that could take four cannon, or two cannon and four machine-guns, as seen here. (Darren Harbar)

Did you know?

In October 1942 an earlier requirement for a Spitfire floatplane was revived and a Spitfire VB was adapted by Folland Aircraft. Three were converted and shipped to the Middle East in 1943, but they saw no action and in early 1944 the whole scheme was abandoned.

With the installation of a Vokes air filter inside a bulky fairing under the nose, the Mk V was the first Spitfire to be 'tropicalised'.
(via Peter Cooper)

and four machine-guns. These 'universal' wings, known as 'C' wings, were fitted to most of the later marks and were recognisable by the projecting mountings for the outer cannon when, as was usually the case, mixed armament was fitted.

The Mk V was the first mark to be 'tropicalised' with the installation of a Vokes air filter inside a bulky fairing under the nose. Although crucial for desert use the filter did not improve the lines of the Spitfire, although it had surprisingly little effect on performance. It also had improved cockpit ventilation and stowage for desert equipment, water and emergency rations behind the cockpit. In Malta an improvised bomb rack was introduced so that a 250lb bomb could be carried under each wing. Later production VCs had extended horn balances and metal-covered ailerons. Some Mk Vs were operated with clipped wing tips.

Did you know?
Wing Commander Douglas Bader, who commanded the Tangmere Fighter Wing during the spring and summer of 1941, had a personal Spitfire VA with the distinctive markings D-B. Bader preferred to engage the enemy from short-range using machine-guns and for a long time resisted having to fly a cannon-fitted aircraft.

Appearing after the Mk IX, the Spitfire VIII had a modified airframe to accept the Merlin 70 with a two-stage super-charger and a retractable tailwheel, as shown on this HF. VIIIC. (Jamie Hunter)

➤

Most pressurised Mk VIIs, of which only 140 were built, were fitted with Merlin 64s with a Marshall Mk XII blower. Wing-tip extensions added 3ft 4in (1.02m) to the span of a Mk V. This F. VII was based in the Orkneys in February 1944. (via Dr Alfred Price)

A total of 6,479 Spitfire Vs were produced (1,367 Mk VAs, 4,477 Mk VBs and 635 Mk VCs) – more than any other variant and nearly 30 per cent of all Spitfires manufactured.

The **Spitfire VI** was a pressurised version developed from the Mk VB and aimed at combating high-flying Junkers Ju 86P/R reconnaissance aircraft. It was powered by a 1,415hp Merlin 47/49 with a four-blade Rotol propeller. The Mk VI had a non-sliding hood with basic pressurisation, but did offer an emergency jettison facility. The wings had extended tips, increasing its span to 40ft 2in. Armament for the 100 aircraft built was comparable to that of the Mk VB. Another

Did you know?

On 12 September 1942 Pilot Officer Emanuel Galetzine, flying one of the specially modified Mk IXs, encountered a Junkers Ju 86R at 43,500ft (well over 8 miles high) over the Isle of Wight. This was the highest recorded combat of the war.

similarly pressurised version was the **Spitfire VII**, of which there were two subvariants. The **F.VII** was powered by the two-speed, two-stage 1,520hp Merlin 60 or 70, while the **HF.VII** had the Merlin 71 with a Bendix injection carburettor. A total of 140 Mk VIIs were built from April 1942.

Appearing after the Mk IX, the **Spitfire VIII** had a redesigned airframe to accept the Merlin with a two-stage supercharger. Three versions were produced, the **F.VIII** with a Merlin 61 or 63 and a standard wing of 36ft 10in span, the **LF.VIII** with a 1,720hp Merlin 66 and the **HF.VIII** with a Merlin 70 and extended wing tips to give a span of 40ft 2in. Among the other improvements on the Mk VIII was the fitting of a retractable tailwheel. A total of 1,658 Spitfire VIIIs were produced, most of which were low-altitude clipped-wing versions; the bulk of these

served in the Middle East, Italy and the Far East. These aircraft were characterised by a large but neat air intake that came fairly far forward under the nose.

In the summer of 1942 it was obvious that the time had come to improve the Spitfire VC's performance, especially with the newly operational German Focke Wulf Fw 190 coming into Luftwaffe service. This was achieved by fitting the Merlin 61 two-stage, two-speed supercharged engine of

'I loved the Spitfire, in all her many versions. But I have to admit that the later marks, although they were faster than the earlier ones, were also much heavier and so did not handle so well. You did not have much positive control over them. One test of manoeuvrability was to throw the Spitfire into a flick roll and see how many times she rolled. With the Mk II or Mk V one got two and a half flick rolls, but the Mk IX was heavier and you got only one and a half. With the later and still heavier versions one got even less.

The essence of aircraft design is compromise, and an improvement at one end of the performance envelope is rarely achieved without a deterioration somewhere else.'

Alex Henshaw, chief test pilot at the Castle Bromwich factory, who personally test flew over 2,000 Spitfires.

1,660hp and a four-blade Rotol propeller into a Mk V airframe, thereby producing the **Spitfire IX**. The bigger Merlin 61 required a longer nose and a new four-blade propeller. It also featured multiple exhaust stubs which replaced the triple ejector type. The inter-cooler for the two-stage supercharger led to the adoption of a revised radiator and oil cooler arrangement. In place of the small circular oil radiator beneath the port wing, a ducted radiator of equal size to that under

The Spitfire IX featured a number of changes to the power-plant, with the two-stage, two-speed supercharged Merlin 61 driving a four-blade propeller; it also had revised underwing radiators.
(Daniel J. March)

the starboard wing was fitted to accommodate both the oil cooler and the intercooler. A heat exchanger was situated on top of the engine. This latest power-plant, developing 70 per cent more horsepower than the original Merlin in the Mk II, enabled the Mk IX to reach 416mph. Early Mk IXs had the 'universal' wing but 1944 saw the introduction of the 'E' wing with higher calibre 0.50in Browning machine-guns. A total of 5,665 Spitfire IXs were built, although it had been intended only as a stop-gap model when introduced in mid-1942.

The **Spitfire PR.X**, of which only sixteen were made, was converted from the Mk II airframe and powered by the Merlin 64.

◄◄
The clipped-wing Spitfire LF.IXE introduced in 1944 featured the 'E' wing with higher calibre 0.50in Browning machine-guns.

◄
Based on the Mk IX, the PR.XI was unpressurised but had cameras in the fuselage, set at a slight angle to the vertical to the rear of the cockpit.

First of the Griffon-engined Spitfires, these Mk XIIs of 41 Squadron had a larger rudder with a pointed tip, retractable tailwheel and Mk V-style radiators.
(via Michael J.F. Bowyer)

A development of the Mk VIII, the Spitfire XIV was powered by a 2,050hp two-stage supercharged Rolls-Royce Griffon 65, driving a five-blade propeller. It also had a longer nose and redesigned fin and rudder.
(Andrew P. March)

It appeared after the Mk IX-based **Spitfire PR.XI**, of which 471 were built. This variant had two cameras located in the rear fuselage. They were in tandem, pointing downwards at a slight angle to the vertical. These cameras were usually of the F52 telephoto type with a 36in focal lens and electrically controlled. They functioned automatically, giving a 60 per cent overlap on all photographs. Special heaters, using exhaust gases, were fitted into the camera bays to prevent the equipment freezing at high altitudes.

The first of the Griffon-engined Spitfires, the **Mk XII** had a larger chord rudder to balance the increased side area forward of the centre of gravity. This rudder was distinctive with a pointed tip. The Mk XII had a two-speed, but not two-stage, supercharger with no intercooler so that the Mk V radiator and oil cooler fairings were used. A retractable tailwheel was fitted to later production aircraft. The first of 100 Mk XIIs was flown in 1941 and went into service the following year.

Only eighteen Spitfire **PR.XIII**s were produced, all converted from Mk VB airframes. This mark was externally similar to the PR.IV but had armament for protection on its low-level photo-reconnaissance work.

The **Spitfire XIV**, of which 1,055 were manufactured, was a development of the Mk VIII with a two-stage supercharged Griffon 65 of 2,050hp fitted with a Coffman starter. The Mk XIV had the 'C' wing armament of two 20mm cannon and two 0.50in machine-guns. Deeper, double radiator

'One of our early problems was to convince the Typhoons at Lympne and Manston that we were on their side. Our clipped wings gave us the appearance of Luftwaffe Focke Wulf Fw 190s and there were several ugly encounters between the Typhoons and ourselves, with us at the receiving end. Fortunately, we could just out-distance a Typhoon provided we saw it in time, otherwise blood would have been spilled.'

Commanding Officer, 41 Squadron

fairings were introduced, while the greater power at altitude was utilised by a five-blade Rotol propeller. Two-stage supercharging resulted in an even longer nose and spinner. To counteract this, together with the increased torque, a completely redesigned fin and rudder of larger area were adopted. A fully retractable tailwheel was standard. Some production XIVs had the 'E' wing and rear vision hood together with a cut-down rear fuselage. The **Mk XIVE** had clipped wings and the **FR.XIV** had oblique cameras in the rear fuselage. The wingspan was 36ft 10in and fuselage length 32ft 8in, and it had a maximum speed in excess of 450mph and a range of 600 miles.

The Mk XIV entered squadron service shortly before D-Day on 6 June 1944 and took part in the invasion of Europe as well as

Some Mk XIVs had the clipped 'E' wing and a revised tear-drop cockpit canopy, together with a cut-down rear fuselage. This FR.XIVE had oblique cameras in the rear fuselage.

Spitfires like this FR.XIVE continued in service with the RAF for six years after the end of the Second World War.

An F.XIVC in Far East Air Force markings. The Mk XIV was the most numerous Griffon-engined Spitfire variant to see wartime service, mainly from bases in Thailand and Indo-China.

Did you know?

On 1 January 1951 Spitfire XVIIIs of 60 Squadron, operating from Singapore, flew a ground-attack sortie against Communist forces in the Malayan jungle. This was the last time RAF pilots flew Spitfire fighters in anger.

combating V1 flying bombs. During the final days of the war the Mk XIV served with the 2nd Tactical Air Force (2TAF) in the Netherlands alongside Typhoons and Tempests and to good effect with squadrons in the Far East. To give increased range a 90-gallon jettisonable fuel tank was carried under the fuselage. The Mk XIV continued in service with RAF units until 1951, when it was finally replaced by Vampires and Meteors.

The last significant fighter variant to be powered by the Merlin was the **Spitfire LF.XVI**, which had the Packard-built 1,750hp Merlin 266. Manufactured in tandem with the Mk IX, the Mk XVI was flown by the 2nd Tactical Air Force, a total of 1,054 being

➤

Packard-built Merlin 266s, developing 1,750hp, were fitted to the LF.XVI, which was manufactured in tandem with the Mk IX. This example carries the black and white striped invasion markings that were applied for the D-Day landing operations in June 1944.
(Daniel J. March)

Did you know?

On 5 February 1952 Flight Lieutenant Ted Powles of 81 Squadron in Hong Kong took his Spitfire PR.XIX on a meteorological flight and reached 51,500ft (9¾ miles), the highest ever attained by a Spitfire. During his descent he recorded a diving speed of Mach 0.94 (690mph).

delivered during 1944–5. The Packard Merlin, produced in the USA at Detroit, was not interchangeable with the British Merlin, resulting in the new designation XVI. Employed as a low-level fighter, the Mk XVI had a four-blade Rotol constant-speed propeller. Armament comprised two 20mm Hispano cannon and two 0.50in machine-guns. As a fighter-bomber it carried two 250lb bombs on external racks beneath the clipped wings. Of the two Mk XVI series, the later batch featured a rear view 'tear-drop' hood and had an additional 66-gallon fuel capacity from two tanks fitted inside the rear fuselage.

Designed in 1944, the **Spitfire XVIII** was developed with strengthened wings, fuselage and undercarriage to cater for additional fuel tanks in the wings and rear fuselage. An FR version with two oblique cameras in the fuselage was originally intended for operations in the Far East as a fighter-reconnaissance aircraft. Only 300 were built as production ceased after VJ-Day. Powered by a Griffon 65, it had a maximum speed of 440mph and an initial rate of climb of 5,045ft/min.

The **Spitfire PR.XIX** was derived from the Mk XIV, with greater fuel capacity and usually a pressurised cockpit with a rounded

➤
Virtually indistinguishable from a late production FR.XIV, with the 'E' wing and bubble canopy, the Spitfire XVIII had a strengthened wing structure and undercarriage to cope with its higher all-up weight.

Over-priming has caused a fiery start-up of this Mk XVIII's Griffon 65 engine. It came too late for wartime service, but six overseas-based RAF squadrons did eventually receive the type.
(Graham Kilsby)

This Spitfire XVIII was fitted with a 'J'-type winch for target-towing trials in 1948.
(via Peter J. Cooper)

windscreen in place of the bulletproof screen. A Griffon 65 or 66 was installed giving a maximum speed of 446mph. First deliveries were made in May 1944, with a total of 225 being built.

The **Spitfire XX** was basically a Mk IV with a Griffon engine but redesignated to avoid confusion with the PR.IV. It was not put into production.

So numerous were the variations in the basic design that the system of giving the mark numbers in Roman numerals was ended. After the Mk XX the variants were numbered in Arabic figures, in common

The Spitfire 20 series had a redesigned and stronger wing, repositioned undercarriage and the Mk XIV's longer nose and tail, and was fitted with four 20mm cannon. In the foreground is an F.22, with an F.21 and F.24 flying alongside.
(via Brian Strickland)

Did you know?

The Spitfire served the RAF through the entire era of the piston-engined monoplane fighter, and at its end the Mk 24 was a match for the best piston-engined fighters being built in the USA and the USSR.

with all types of aircraft then entering RAF service.

First produced in 1945, the **Spitfire F.21, F.22** and **F.24** marked the final development of the land-based fighter aircraft. The Mk 21 entered service shortly before the end of the war. It had a redesigned, stronger wing, the Mk XIV's longer nose and tail, and a repositioned undercarriage and was fitted with four 20mm cannon. The Mks 22 and 24 were subvariants developed after the end of the war, the last F.24 leaving the South Marston factory in February 1948.

These final marks of Spitfires, all Griffon-engined, broke with the elliptical wing shape by having a completely new laminar flow wing with a revised planform, together with larger ailerons. Most of the final batch of Spitfires had a modified fin and rudder developed for the Spiteful. The Mk 24 was a long-range version with extra fuel tanks in the rear fuselage. The Griffon 61 and 64 developed 2,035hp and drove five-blade Rotol constant-speed airscrews with diameter increased to 11ft, thereby necessitating longer undercarriage oleo legs to improve ground clearance. It had become evident that

Powered by a 2,035hp Griffon 61/64, the Mk 24, the last of the RAF's Spitfires, was a long-range version with extra fuel tanks in the rear fuselage.

> The Spitfire F.21, with its new-shape laminar flow wing, entered service shortly before the end of the war. (via Peter J. Cooper)

Did you know?

The all-up weight of the last operational mark of Spitfire to enter service was equivalent to a Mk I of 1938 taking off with thirty-two airline passengers and all their baggage on board!

20mm ammunition was the only really effec-
tive type, and the redesigned wings housed
four 20mm Hispano cannon, each with
140 rounds of ammunition per gun; these
were made standard on the Mks 21, 22 and
24. The bulky blisters stayed to the end in
spite of design efforts on Supermarine's part.

In 1946 the manufacturer converted a
Mk VIII (MT818) into the prototype two-seat
trainer. Known as the Spitfire T.8, with the
company designation Type 509, it carried the
civil registration G-AIDN. Subsequently about
25 Mk IXs were converted for overseas sales
as two-seat **Spitfire T.9** trainers.

Carolyn Grace's well-known Spitfire T.9 was a former Irish Air Corps aircraft, but it has a lower rear cockpit canopy compared with the raised original.

In 1941 the Fleet Air Arm's urgent need for a fighter with modern performance was first met by the introduction of the Spitfire. A Mk V fitted with a deck arrester hook and catapult spools made the first take-offs and landings on HMS *Illustrious*. The Admiralty asked for 400 converted VCs, but in the event only 48 VBs and 202 VCs were actually produced. The first 'hooked' Spitfire was a Mk VB, which first flew at Worthy Down in January 1942. It was later known as the **Seafire I**. On 7 March 1942 fifteen Spitfire VBs made the celebrated

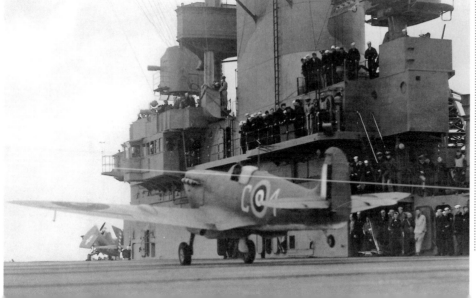

◄
A Spitfire VB leaves the deck of the US carrier Wasp in March 1942. It was en route to Malta to assist with the critical defence of the island.

flight off HMS *Eagle* in the Mediterranean, east of Gibraltar, to the island of Malta. Two subsequent fly-offs were undertaken from the US carrier *Wasp*, which Prime Minister Winston Churchill had personally arranged to 'borrow'.

A prototype **Seafire II** was first flown in February 1942. It was generally similar to the Seafire Mk I with catapult spools and strengthened undercarriage and fuselage, and was powered by a 1,645hp Merlin 32 driving a four-blade propeller. A low-level fighter version, the **Seafire IIC** was also produced.

The first folding-wing development was the **Seafire III**, the prototype of which took to the air in November 1943. The folding wings were an ingenious adaptation of the original one-piece wing. The main hinge was on the torsion box spar and only light-weight fittings held the rear part of the wing

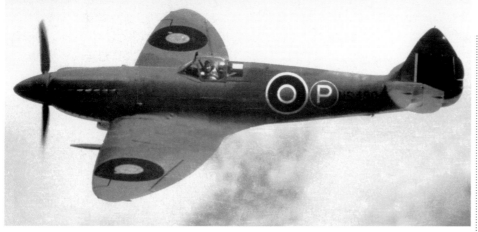

together. The wing tips folded separately to reduce the height. The first production versions reached 894 Squadron in November 1943. Subvariants produced included the **LF.III** with a 1,585hp Merlin 55M and the **FR.III** equipped with two F24 cameras.

The first Griffon-engined version was the **Seafire F.XV**, which was basically a Mk III with a Spitfire Mk XII power-plant. The proto-type was first flown in February 1944, with service deliveries following in September. Improved engine performance from the Griffon VI gave the **Seafire Mk XVII** a maximum speed of 411mph when it entered service with 883 Squadron in September 1945.

Three final variants, the **Seafire F.45, F.46** and **F.47**, followed after the war had ended. The Seafire F.45 and F.46 were 'hooked'

➤
Entering service after the war, the Seafire XVII eventually became the longest-lived of the Seafires, remaining in service with RNVR and training squadrons.

Spitfire F.21/22s, while the F.47 was a fully navalised version of the F.22, with folding wings. All had the 'tear-drop' cockpit canopy and were fitted with four 20mm cannon. The F.45 was powered by a Griffon 61 while the F.46 featured a Griffon 85 driving a Rotol contra-rotating propeller. Thus the Seafire became the first operational naval aircraft to be fitted with 'contra-props'. This reduced torque effect while the extra blade area improved take-off thrust, both being important features on carrier-borne aircraft.

The **Seafire F.47** had the even more powerful Griffon 87/88. It had an increase in fin and rudder area as well as larger tailplane and elevators. The wing-folding design was new, with only the outer wing section folding upwards under hydraulic power. Another feature of the F.47 was increased fuel capacity both internally and in external drop tanks. Of

the ninety Seafire F.47s built, a number saw active service after the war in Malaya and Korea. Total Seafire production had reached 2,622 aircraft when production ended in March 1949.

With the introduction of the laminar flow wing there were no further marks of Spitfire/Seafire after the F.24/F.47 respectively, as the subsequent developments were renamed Spiteful and Seafang.

The ultimate Seafire – the F.47 was faster, heavier and more versatile, and was the last to see active service in Malaya and Korea.

There are, in 2006, many examples of the veteran warbird on display around the world, and significantly as many as fifty Spitfires in airworthy condition or nearing the end of restoration to fly. In the UK the RAF Battle of Britain Memorial Flight has a Mk IIa, a Mk V, a Mk IX and a pair of Mk XIXs operating from RAF Coningsby, Lincolnshire. At the Imperial War Museum Airfield at Duxford in Cambridgeshire, the Fighter Collection, Historic Flying Ltd, the Aircraft Restoration Company, the Old Flying Machine Company (OFMC), Spitfire Ltd and several individual owners have a further twelve Spitfires that

This Spitfire FR.XVIII (SM845) is owned by Historic Flying Ltd at Duxford.

The Historic Aircraft Collection's Spitfire VB (BM597) landing at Duxford.

are flown regularly. Seventy years after its first flight the Supermarine Spitfire lives on. No longer in the front line of the Royal Air Force, they entertain us at airshows and provide a vivid reminder of the heroic achievements of 'The Few' during the dark days of the Battle of Britain and the courage of the fighter pilots in the following years of the Second World War.

➤
Griffon quartet: FR.XIVE leading FR.XVIIIE, another FR.XIVE and a PR.XIX in a Duxford airshow flypast.

The RAF Battle of Britain Memorial Flight, today based at RAF Coningsby in Lincolnshire, has been flying Spitfires since it was formed at RAF Biggin Hill in July 1957, initially as the Historic Aircraft Flight with three Spitfire PR.XIXs (PM631, PS853 and PS915) and one Hurricane.

In October 1957 three Spitfire XVIs (TE330, TE476 and SL574) joined the Flight, but two years later TE476 and SL574 were

Spitfire IIA P7350 was restored for the Battle of Britain film and was subsequently acquired by the Battle of Britain Memorial Flight.

'During the Battle of Britain, I often used spins in the Spitfire to save my life. I can think of at least four times when this simple but dramatic manoeuvre of pretending to be shot down came in handy. I used it when I was attacked by German fighters and had no chance to fight successfully. I usually started with a snap roll, which culminated in a vertical stabilised spin. I would quickly close and open the throttle, producing black smoke from the engine exhaust.'

Jan Zurakowski, chief test pilot of Avro Canada after the war and a well-known aerobatic pioneer

retired from service after accidents and TE330 went to the Smithsonian Institute in the USA. Spitfire VB AB910 was donated by Vickers-Armstrong in 1965 and in 1968 Spitfire IIA P7350 was added after it had been restored for the film *Battle of Britain*.

One of the original Mk XIXs, PS853, was sold in January 1994 to defray the cost of rebuilding Hawker Hurricane LF363, which had been damaged in an accident. In November 1997 the Flight added Spitfire IX MK356, formerly at the St Athan Museum Collection. Two non-flying Spitfire XVIs (TE311 and TB382) have been allocated to the Flight for spares support/recovery, one of which might be restored to fly.

The Battle of Britain Memorial Flight's fighters in the 1970s. (Bottom to top): Spitfire V, Spitfire IIA, two Hurricanes and two Spitfire XIXs. (via R.L. Ward)

Spitfire LF.IXE MK356 is
the most recent addition
to the Battle of Britain
Memorial Flight's fighters
at Coningsby.

The following Spitfires and Seafires are in airworthy condition or under active restoration to fly in the foreseeable future (denoted by an asterisk *).

SPITFIRES

P7350	IIA	Battle of Britain Memorial Flight, RAF Coningsby, Lincs.
AB910	LF.VB	Battle of Britain Memorial Flight, RAF Coningsby, Lincs.
AR213*	IA	Sheringham Aviation UK Ltd, Booker, Bucks.
AR501	LF.VC	Shuttleworth Collection, Old Warden, Beds.
AR614	F.VC	Flying Heritage Collection, Seattle, Washington, USA
BM597	F.VB	Historic Aircraft Collection, Duxford, Cambs.
EN398	HF.IXE	TAM/Wings of Dream Museum, Sao Carlos, Brazil
EP120	LF.VB	The Fighter Collection, Duxford, Cambs.
JG891*	LF.VC	Historic Flying Ltd, Duxford, Cambs.
MH434	LF.IXB	The Old Flying Machine Company, Duxford, Cambs.
MJ627	T.9	Maurice Bayliss, East Kirkby, Lincs.
MJ730	LF.IXE	The Fighter Factory, Suffolk County, New York, USA
MJ772	LF.IX	Museum of Flight, Seattle-Boeing Field, Washington, USA
MK356	LF.IXE	Battle of Britain Memorial Flight, RAF Coningsby, Lincs.
MK732	LF.IXC	Royal Netherlands Air Force Historic Flight, Gilze Rijen AB, Netherlands
MK912	LF.IXC	Ed Russell, Niagara South, Ontario, Canada
MK923	LF.IXE	Museum of Flight, Seattle-Boeing Field, Washington, USA
MK959	LF.IXE	Raybourne Thompson, Houston, Texas, USA

Mk IA AR213 has been operated by Personal Plane Services at Wycombe Air Park on behalf of its owners for many years.

ML407	T.9	Carolyn Grace, Duxford, Cambs.
ML417	LF.IXC	Tom Friedkin, Chino Warbird Inc., Chino, California, USA
MT719	LF.VIIIC	Cavanaugh Flight Museum, Dallas-Addison, Texas, USA
MT818	T.8	Jack Erickson, Tillamook, Oregon, USA
MT928	HF.VIIIC	Robert Lamplough, Filton, South Glos.
MV239	HF.VIIIC	David Lowy/Temora Aviation Museum, Temora, New South Wales, Australia
MV268	FR.XIVE	The Fighter Collection, Duxford, Cambs.
NH631	LF.VIIIC	Indian Air Force Historic Flight, Palam Air Base, New Delhi, India
NH749	LF.XIVE	David Price/Commemorative Air Force, Camarillo, California, USA
NH799	FR.XIV	Aviation Trading Company, Ardmore, New Zealand
NH904	FR.XIVC	Pond Warbirds, Palm Springs Air Museum, Palm Springs, California, USA
PL344	LF.IXE	Tom Blair, Bartow, Florida, USA
PL965	PR.XI	Peter Teichman, North Weald, Essex
PM631	PR.XIX	Battle of Britain Memorial Flight, RAF Coningsby, Lincs.
PS853	PR.XIX	Rolls-Royce plc, Filton, South Glos.
PS890	PR.XIX	Christophe Jacquard, Dijon, France
PS915	PR.XIX	Battle of Britain Memorial Flight, RAF Coningsby, Lincs.
PT462	T.9	Anthony Hodgson, Dragon Flight, Caernarfon, North Wales
RM689*	F.XIV	Rolls-Royce plc, Filton, South Glos.
RN201	FR.XIVE	Historic Flying Ltd, Duxford, Cambs.
RR232*	HF.IXC	Martin Phillips, Exeter, Devon

RW386*	LF.XVIE	Historic Flying Ltd, Duxford, Cambs.
SL721	LF.XVIE	Michael Potter, Gatineau, Quebec, Canada
SM520*	T.9	Paul Portelli, Thruxton, Hants.
SM832	F.XIVC	Tom Friedkin, Chino Warbird Inc., Chino, California, USA
SM845	FR.XVIIIE	Historic Flying Ltd, Duxford, Cambs.
SM969*	FR.XVIIIE	Wizzard Investments Ltd, North Weald, Essex
TA805*	HF.IX	Peter Monk, Duxford, Cambs.
TB863	LF.XVIE	New Zealand Fighter Pilots Museum, Wanaka, New Zealand
TD248	LF.XVIE	Spitfire Ltd, Duxford, Cambs.
TE184	LF.XVIE	Alain de Cadenet, Duxford, Cambs.
TE308	T.9	Bill Greenwood, Aspen, Colorado, USA
TE311*	LF.XVIE	Battle of Britain Memorial Flight, RAF Coningsby, Lincs.
TE356	LF.XVIE	Evergreen Aviation Museum, McMinnville, Oregon, USA
TE392	LF.XVIE	Lone Star Flight Museum, Galveston, Texas, USA
TE476	LF.XVIE	Kermit Weeks, Fantasy of Flight, Polk City, Florida, USA
TE554	LF.IXE	Israeli Air Force Museum, Hatzerim AB, Israel
TP280	FR.XVIIIE	Frasca Air Museum, Champaign, Illinois, USA
TZ138	FR.XIVE	Robert Jens, Vancouver, British Columbia, Canada
IAC161	T.9	Historic Flying Ltd, Duxford, Cambs.

SEAFIRES

SX336*	F.XVII	Tim J. Manna, North Weald, Essex
VP441	FR.47	James E. Smith, Kalispell, Montana, USA

Did you know?
The power of the Spitfire's Rolls-Royce Merlin engines increased from 1,000hp in 1936 to over 1,700hp in 1944. The larger Griffon increased from 1,735hp in 1941 to 2,350hp in 1945. In both cases the increases were achieved primarily by improvements in supercharge technology.

◄
Donated by Rolls-Royce in 2002, this Spitfire HF.IXE (EN398) is airworthy at Sao Carlos, Brazil. (Frank B. Mormillo)

87

EP120

Did you know?

Of 1,185 enemy aircraft shot down by the RAF's two principal fighters in the Battle of Britain, Spitfire squadrons shot down 44.6 per cent and Hurricanes 55.4 per cent. Of Luftwaffe aircraft shot down by Hurricanes, 66.2 per cent were bombers – for Spitfires, only 46.7 per cent were bombers.

First flown after restoration at East Midlands Airport in November 1988, Spitfire LF.IXE MJ730 was sold to Jerry Yagen in the USA ten years later.

Seen here while operating with the Dutch Spitfire Flight, LF.IXC MK732 is now owned by the Royal Netherlands Air Force Historic Flight and repainted in RNethAF markings. (Richard Paver)

Owned by The Fighter Collection at Duxford for twenty years, Spitfire LF.IXC ML417 is now at Chino, California, with the Planes of Fame.
(Frank B. Mormillo)

Did you know?

American pilots flew Spitfires in the RAF 'Eagle' Squadrons in 1940–2 and in the US Army Air Force in North Africa in 1942–3.

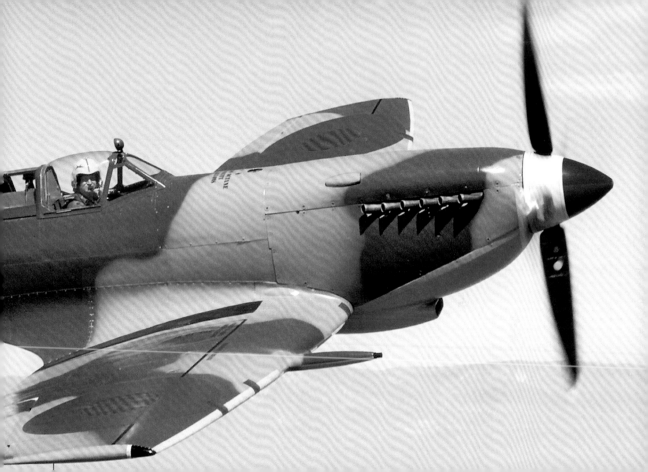

This Spitfire LF.IXC (MK912) was restored by Historic Flying Ltd and first flown in September 2000. It is now owned by Ed Russell in Ontario, Canada.

Spitfire LF.VIIIC MT719 photographed over Middle Wallop, Hants, before it was sold to the Cavanaugh Flight Museum in Dallas, USA.

▶
Robs Lamplough's Spitfire HF.VIIIC MT928 at low level at Filton, where it is based.

▶▶
The Fighter Collection's clipped-wing Spitfire FR.XIVE airborne at Duxford.

Did you know?
On 27 April 1944 high-speed diving trials were conducted with a Spitfire at Farnborough. Squadron Leader 'Marty' Martindale reached a true air speed of 606mph (Mach 0.89) in Mk XI EN409, but then lost his propeller.

► Spitfire LF.XIVE NH749 is based with the Southern California Wing of the Commemorative Air Force at Camarillo.
(Frank B. Mormillo)

►► Flown in the UK as scarlet-painted G-FIRE, Spitfire FR.XIVC NH904 is now with the Palm Springs Air Museum in California.
(Frank B. Mormillo)

Owned by Frenchman Christophe Jacquard, this Griffon-powered Mk XIX PS890 has contra-rotating propellers like the Seafire 47.

Did you know?

In 1943 some Air Sea Rescue squadrons began to receive Spitfire IIs equipped to drop a dinghy, food and medicine packs to ditched aircrew. The Spitfire could defend itself while waiting for a Supermarine Walrus and then escort it home.

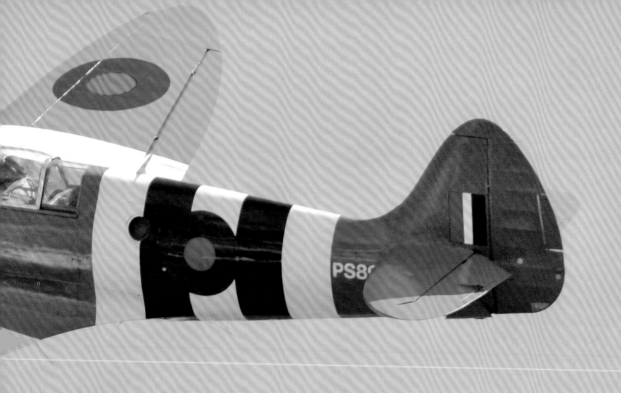

Anthony Hodgson's two-seat Spitfire T.9 PT462.
(Paul Harrison)

Once displayed at the Beaulieu Motor Museum, Hants, Spitfire LF.XVIE SL721 is now in Canada.
(Frank B. Mormillo)

First Seafire to be restored to fly in the UK, Tim Manna's Mk XVII SX336, was nearing completion at North Weald in December 2005.

Did you know?

The last Spitfire to be 'presented' was Mk IX TB900 on 19 March 1945, fittingly named *Winston Churchill*. By the end of the war donations for Spitfires had totalled around £14 million (about £175 million in present-day values).

Taking off for a display at Shoreham, West Sussex, in September 2005, this LF.XVIE is owned by Spitfire Ltd at Duxford.
(Ben Dunnell)

John Romain taxiing Spitfire IX TA805 at Duxford for its first flight on 7 December 2005.
(All photographs on this page by Col Pope)

Taking off . . .

. . . and flying by.

APPENDIX I – SPECIFICATION

SPITFIRE I

Engine:	Rolls-Royce Merlin II/III
Power:	1,030hp
Max speed:	362mph (584km/h)
Length:	29ft 11in (9.1m)
Wingspan:	36ft 10in (11.23m)
Height:	11ft 5in (3.48m)
Armament:	
Machine-guns	8 x 0.303in
Cannon	–
Max all-up weight:	5,800lb (2,631kg)
Range:	395 miles (636km)
Number built:	1,583
Entered service:	1938

SPITFIRE IX

Engine:	Rolls-Royce Merlin III
Power:	1,565hp
Max speed:	408mph (657km/h)
Length:	31ft 0.5in (9.45m)
Wingspan:	36ft 10in (11.23m)
Height:	11ft 8in (3.56m)
Armament:	
Machine-guns	4 x 0.303in
Cannon	2 x 20mm
Max all-up weight:	7,500lb (3,402kg)
Range:	434 miles (698km)
Number built:	5,665
Entered service:	1942

SPITFIRE XIV

Engine:	Rolls-Royce Griffon 65/67
Power:	2,035hp
Max speed:	439mph (706.5km/h)
Length:	32ft 8in (9.96m)
Wingspan:	36ft 10in (11.23m)
Height:	11ft 8.25in (3.56m)
Armament:	
Machine-guns	2 x 0.5in
Cannon	2 x 20mm
Max all-up weight:	8,475lb (3,843kg)
Range:	465 miles (748km)
Number built:	957
Entered service:	1944

SPITFIRE F24

Engine:	Rolls-Royce Griffon 61
Power:	2,035hp
Max speed:	450mph (724km/h)
Length:	32ft 8in (9.96m)
Wingspan:	36ft 11in (11.25m)
Height:	11ft 9.75in (3.6m)
Armament:	
Machine-guns	–
Cannon	4 x 20mm
Max all-up weight:	9,182lb (4,165kg)
Range:	580 miles (935km)
Number built:	54
Entered service:	1946

APPENDIX II – SPITFIRE MILESTONES

1928   Supermarine's Works at Southampton taken over by Vickers; R.J. Mitchell appointed director and chief designer (post held until his death in 1937).

1931   Mitchell's Supermarine S6B seaplane, powered by the Rolls-Royce 'R' engine, wins the Schneider Trophy outright.

1934   November: Mitchell receives permission to proceed with the design of a PV.12-powered Type 300 fighter.

1935   The Air Ministry, recognising the potential of Mitchell's design, issues an initial contract, written around Mitchell's design, for the production of one prototype at a cost of £11,930.

1936   5 March: Maiden flight of prototype Spitfire K5054, at Eastleigh, Hants.

1936   3 June: Supermarine receives its first order for 310 Spitfires (to the value of £1.25m sterling) and production begins.

1936   28 July: The name 'Spitfire' approved by the Air Ministry.

1936   The Rolls-Royce PV.12, now named the Merlin, completes its service test at 975hp.

1937   11 June: Death of Spitfire designer R.J. Mitchell, aged 42, just fifteen months after the Spitfire first flew. He had suffered from cancer since 1933.

1938   14 May: The first production Spitfire, K9787, flies at Eastleigh and is delivered to Martlesham Heath on 27 July for trials.

1938   4 August: First Spitfire I (K9792) delivered to 19 Squadron at RAF Duxford, to replace the Gauntlet biplane.

1938	October: Supermarine Aviation Works (Vickers) Ltd, with its parent company Vickers (Aviation) Ltd, taken over by Vickers-Armstrong Ltd.
1939	3 September: At the outbreak of war a total of 1,960 Spitfires were on order, of which 306 Mk Is had been delivered to 10 squadrons of the RAF (Nos 19, 41, 54, 65, 66, 72, 74, 602, 603 and 611).
1939	16 October: Spitfires in action for the first time when 602 and 603 Squadrons engage Luftwaffe bombers off the coast of Scotland, en route to attack Royal Navy warships in the Firth of Forth. Two Junkers Ju 88s shot down.
1939	18 November: The first of two Spitfire PR.1Cs, unarmed and with a 5-in focal length vertically mounted camera in each wing, flies the first Spitfire PR mission.
1940	12 May: Spitfire fighters mount their first operation over Europe.
1940	18/19 June: The first occasion on which a Luftwaffe bomber was shot down by a Spitfire flying at night.
1940	July: At the start of the Battle of Britain nearly 1,000 Spitfires were on the strength of 19 RAF squadrons.
1940	24 and 26 September: Woolston and Itchen Works bombed in daylight raids. Supermarine manufacture is subsequently dispersed over a wide area of the south of England and production begins in garages and other small units requisitioned by the Ministry of Aircraft Production.
1940	December: Maiden flight of the first prototype Spitfire V (K9788), which was introduced as a stop-gap between the Mk II and Mk III.

1941	15 January: The leading Fighter Command ace of the Second World War, J.E. 'Johnnie' Johnson, claims his first of thirty-four kills in a Spitfire on this day.
1941	27 August: Pilot Officer W. Dunn of 71 'Eagle' Squadron becomes the first American ace of the war by shooting down two Messerschmitt Bf 109Fs in Spitfire IIA P7308.
1941	September: The Admiralty finally obtains permission to acquire the 'Sea Spitfire'.
1941	November: First flight of Seafire IV DP845 (later redesignated as the Mk XX), the first Griffon-powered Seafire.
1941	31 December: By the end of the year, almost every day-fighter squadron in RAF Fighter Command had re-equipped with the more powerful Merlin 45-engined Spitfire V.
1942	7 March: The Mk V becomes the first Spitfire variant to serve overseas as aircraft rushed to Malta to help defend the strategically important Mediterranean island. Soon after they were issued to units in North Africa with 145 Squadron.
1942	15 June: First Seafire IB taken on charge by the Fleet Air Arm.
1942	July: The first Spitfire IXs sent to 64 Squadron at RAF Hornchurch.
1942	19 August: The Dieppe landings in northern France, supported by forty-eight squadrons of Spitfires. They suffered their heaviest single day's loss ever – fifty-nine Spitfires lost to enemy action out of total Allied losses of ninety-seven aircraft.
1942	29 September: The RAF's 71, 121 and 133 Spitfire 'Eagle' Squadrons, flown by American volunteers, transfer to the USAAF.

1942	October: HMS *Furious*, with 801 Squadron on board, becomes the first carrier to take the Seafire into action.
1943	February: The Mk XII enters service with 41 Squadron (and later 91 Squadron) at RAF High Ercall.
1943	8 June: First Seafire III (LR766) delivered to the FAA at Worthy Down; 1,263 examples of this variant were built by Westlands and Cunliffe-Owen.
1943	November: The Seafire III, the first to feature folding wings, enters service with 894 Squadron.
1944	April: The Mk XIV follows the Mk XII into service as another 'interim' type, pending the arrival of the 'Griffon-Spitfire'.
1944	May: The Griffon-engined PR.XIX introduced.
1944	6 June: On D-Day the RAF's Order of Battle included fifty-five squadrons of Spitfire fighters, together with four Air Sea Rescue squadrons which had some Spitfires.
1944	September: The Mk XVI enters service. This had an identical airframe to the Mk IX, but was fitted with an American Packard-built Merlin 266 (equivalent to the 'low-level' Merlin 66).
1944	29 December: A Spitfire IXE of 411 Squadron RCAF, operating in Holland, shoots down five enemy fighters within two minutes – a record for both the RCAF and the RAF.
1945	14 February: A Spitfire XIV of 610 Squadron is the first Spitfire to shoot down one of the new German Me 262 jet fighters, near Munster.

1946   January: Mk VIII MT818/G-AIDN converted as a two-seat trainer. Some twenty-five examples of the Mk IX were converted for overseas sales as the T.9.

1948   January: No 80 becomes the only squadron to receive the Spitfire Mk 24, while based at Gutersloh in Germany; the squadron then moved to Kai Tak in Hong Kong in 1949.

1948   20 February: The last of the 22,758 Spitfire variants built (Mk 24 VN496) delivered by Vickers Supermarine.

1948   May: Declaration of the Malayan Emergency. The RAF deploys FR.XVIIIs of 28 and 60 Squadrons, together with PR.XIXs of 81 Squadron.

1948–9   Spitfire Mk IXs and XVIs acquired from the RAF used against Communist targets in Athens and elsewhere during the Greek civil war.

1949   28 February: Spitfires use 20lb fragmentation bombs for the first time against Malayan terrorists. Over 1,800 operational sorties were flown against terrorists by Spitfires.

1949   March: The final Seafire F.47 delivered to the Fleet Air Arm.

1950   July: Seafire F.47s of 800 Naval Air Squadron from HMS *Triumph* take part in the Korean War.

1951   1 January: The last RAF Spitfire offensive sorties flown by FR.XVIIIs of 81 Squadron.

1951   The last Spitfires with Royal Auxiliary Air Force squadrons withdrawn from service.

1954   1 April: PR.XIX PS888 flies the last operational sortie by an RAF Spitfire, operating from RAF Seletar during the Malayan campaign.

1954   23 November: The last Seafires withdrawn from Fleet Air Arm service with 764 Naval Air Squadron based at RNAS Yeovilton, Somerset.

1955   21 April: The last Spitfire sortie in Hong Kong, as a Hong Kong Auxiliary Air Force F.24 participates in the Queen's Birthday flypast.

1957   9 July: The final trio of PR.XIXs serving with the 'weather' THUM Flight at RAF Woodvale retire and join the RAF Historic Aircraft Flight at Biggin Hill.

1963   One PR.XIX briefly reactivated by the Central Fighter Establishment to assist in the training of Lightning pilots ahead of possible deployment to Indonesia.

TA805 is brought back in to land by John Romain after a successful first flight at Duxford on 7 December 2005.
(Both photographs on this page by Col Pope)